Practical Keys To Knowing Christ To Walk In Deliverance, Purpose & Destiny

(Revised)

———————

Shallaywa Varita Collie

Revised Edition, 2020
ISBN 978-0-578-65436-2
First Published 2014, First Revision 2019

Published by:
Majestic Priesthood Publication, Freeport, Grand Bahama, Bahamas.
Email: mpppublications@gmail.com

1-242-559-2138

Printed in the United States of America

Acknowledgements & Dedication

Oh Lord my God, I sought you with all my heart and soul and I am complete now that I have found you.

To all my intercessors and my husband and son, may God be with you always.

To my family and Kingdom Apostolic Ministries International family, there is strength in unity.

To my Grandmother Varita Singh, gone too soon

Table of Contents

Why This Book Was Written

As follow-up to "let the word of Christ dwell in you richly in all wisdom…," Colossians 3:16, this book is to magnify the importance of knowing Christ Jesus and making Him known. Follow the author as she expounds on her journey of getting to know Christ and search the scriptures passages to uncover how they relate to everyday life, and the importance of living as a kingdom citizen.

Examine yourself, your walk, your relationship, and the confidence in Christ you serve. Lift up your head oh you gates and you everlasting doors. Open your eyes, ears, heart and let the King of glory in. What would you do afterwards but to serve Him faithfully. Through writing this book, it is my hope that the word of God, which is living and active, transforms your life and starts to work within you right away. I as well hope that you see God's character revealed in its fullness and believe in Him even more.

PSALM 27

The LORD is my light and my salvation;

Whom shall I fear?

The LORD is the strength of my life;

Of whom shall I be afraid?

When the wicked came against me

To eat up my flesh,

My enemies and foes,

They stumbled and fell.——

Though an army may encamp against me,

My heart shall not fear;

Though war may rise against me,

In this I will be confident.

one thing I have desired of the LORD,

That will I seek:

That I may dwell in the house of the LORD

All the days of my life,

To behold the beauty of the LORD,

And to inquire in his temple. For in the time of trouble,

He shall hide me in his pavilion;

In the secret place of his tabernacle

He shall hide me;

He shall set me high upon a rock.

And now my head shall be lifted up above my

Enemies all around me;

Therefore I will offer sacrifices of joy in his tabernacle;

I will sing, yes, I will sing praises to the LORD.

Hear, O LORD, when I cry with my voice! Have mercy

also upon me, and answer me.

When you said, "seek my face,"

My heart said to you, "your face, LORD, I will seek."

Do not hide your face from me;

Do not turn your servant away in anger;

You have been my help;

Do not leave me nor forsake me,

O God of my salvation. When my father and my

mother forsake me,

Then the LORD will take care of me.

Teach me your way, O LORD,

And lead me in a smooth path, because of my enemies.

Do not deliver me to the will of my adversaries;

For false witnesses have risen against me,

And such as breathe out violence. I would have lost

heart, unless I had believed

That I would see the goodness of the LORD

In the land of the living.

Wait on the LORD;

Be of good courage,

And he shall strengthen your heart;

Wait, I say, on the LORD

I

MY STORY

When I surrendered to God and began to study His word and dedicated myself to His way, I was transformed. Prior to that supernatural experience, with insecurity and a false sense of importance, I was serving the Lord in the areas of church administration, ushering, finance, children ministry, youth ministry, praise team and protocol. With true commitment of heart and mind, deliverance from evil, dedication to the Lord, and by the power of His Holy Spirit, I am now doing street evangelism, and worldwide crusades and evangelism. The Lord by His grace leads me to give words of knowledge, prophecy, and grants me wisdom of deliverance ministry, plus a unique gifting for preaching and teaching the word of God. You can do this too. Only apply these principles that I have learned. Some of these principles are gleaned from the experiences of seasoned men and women of God, and others from my own knowledge and experiences, and from the Holy Ghost.

It is time to break free from the life you build on a love that was not God's way and confidence as it relates to beauty, power, education, relationships, and money. Without seeking first the Kingdom of God, they will all fail you at one point or the other unless the foundation is in God.

As you read, ask yourselves the following questions:

Am I walking in the purpose and destiny of God?

Where is my confidence, did I build it in Christ?

Am I really saved and delivered by Christ even though I'm fully involved in church activities?

Do my career, practice, church activities, and life really glorify Christ?

Am I impacting others for Christ or is it just about me?

II

GETTING TO KNOW JESUS

Through Trials...

There are two kingdoms that are at war as far as Christianity is concerned to you and me. They are the Kingdom of God which brings eternal life, light and victory, and the kingdom of Satan which brings death (for it kills, steals and destroys). Satan and his wicked hosts plan to separate us from God so that we fail to come into our fullness and feel as though God is a God that is far from us and that we should not pray or seek Him. But the God of love gave us a chance to accept the Lord Jesus as our Savior, so that we might be set free from sin (death, perversion) and have eternal life through Him, being free from spiritual and physical struggles. Through His death, He destroyed him that had the power of death, that is, the devil (Hebrews 2:14).

"I am he that liveth, and was dead; and, behold, I am alive for evermore, Amen; and have the keys of hell and of death." (Rev 1:18)

"In the beginning was the Word, and the Word was with God, and the Word was God...The Word became flesh and made his dwelling among us. We have seen his glory, the glory of the one and only Son, who came from the Father, full of grace and truth." (John 1:1, 1:14)

The story of the Israelites leaving Egypt and going through the wilderness is a perfect example of knowing God. We see here that sometimes God puts us in a place where we have to depend on Him and Him alone. In Exodus 6:6-7, the LORD says, *"I am the LORD; I will bring you out from under the burdens of the Egyptians, I will rescue you from their bondage, and I will redeem you with an outstretched arm and with great judgments. I will take you as my people, and I will be your God. Then you shall know that I am the LORD your God who brings you out from under the burdens of the Egyptians."* There is no difference between the God who delivered the Israelites out of Egypt thousands of years ago and the God who can deliver you and me from any circumstances today. The people of the Bible might have engaged mostly in physical battles at that time such as, wars between kingdoms (e.g. the Kings; King David and his generals); and daily challenges with wicked people who were dwelling among them, who wished to destroy them or convert them into idolaters.

However, in our walk at this present time, though we may endure physical dilemmas such as sickness, lack and strife, our battles are of a spiritual nature. The Bible tells us in Ephesians 6:12 that *"we wrestle not against flesh and blood, but against principalities, against powers, against the rulers of the darkness of this world, and against spiritual wickedness in high places."*

This indicates that as Christians, we are engaged in a war; this war is against the forces of evil that are spirits in nature and in operation. A person may carry out whatever action in the spirit of love, hate, jealousy, patience, kindness; for example. No wonder the

Scripture says you have to pray for those who despitefully use you and against the spiritual attacks of the enemy. There is a spirit behind everything that takes place in the earth, and every human action is a function of his inner self and external influences. Remember Satan once influenced Peter's mind to speak against God's will for Jesus, but knowing the force behind the utterance, Jesus rebuked the enemy rather than get offensive at Peter himself. Proverbs 23:7 says, *"As he thinks in his heart so is he, eat and drink he says but his heart is not with you."*

I want to believe Peter felt embarrassed but kept mute. Yet that incident must have opened his mind to knowing he was at the center of two kingdoms; one wanted to destroy him, the other wanted to help develop his spiritual sensitiveness to God. It thus suggests that the struggles of life can cause us to pull over, get off our vehicle of self, and draw near to the Lord. All the experiences of Israelites in Egypt and in the wilderness come with one objective — knowing the

God of their fathers. And out of this objective comes a nation, a kingdom

Know that the devil doesn't want you to be intimate with God. So when the going becomes challenging, be not dismayed, there is a wave of comfort because the Holy Bible also tells us in 2 Corinthians 10:4 that *"the weapons of our warfare are not carnal, but mighty through God to the pulling down of strong holds,"* for the battle is not yours (2 Chronicles 20:15). Do not be afraid. Stand firm and you will see the deliverance the LORD will bring you today (Exodus 14:13). Situations and circumstances may occur but we must prove to our Lord that we give Him all the power and truly surrender to Him in all things. Thus, we should not compromise our belief or bargain with the devil or half-way believe what the Lord has said to us. We should continue to ask the Lord in faith without wavering, whatever it is we desire according to His will. Anyone that is unstable and unreliable is synonymous to a wave of the sea driven with the wind and tossed.

Attacks from the enemy, cares of this life, struggles, pains, and whatsoever should not draw us away from the Lord, but rather make us run to Him. We shouldn't become unstable because of these things. Jesus and His disciples were rocked by the stormy Sea of Galilee, but after the calm, those timid men came face to face with a new revelation of Jesus — they had a lively experience of God's goodness as to how He saves from destruction.

"For let not that man thinks that he shall receive any thing of the LORD…. A double minded man is unstable in all his ways." (James 1:7-8)

We need to know this. God is the same yesterday, today and forever. Once we call on the name of the Lord when things happen, we shall be saved, for it is neither by our might, nor our power, but it is by the Spirit of the Lord; to those who truly are in God. Why, because the Lord wants to know that you trust Him and He needs to be able to trust you as well.

"I know also, my God, that you test the heart and have pleasure in uprightness. As for me, in the uprightness of my heart I have willingly offered all these things; and now with joy I have seen your people, who are present here to offer willingly to you." (1 Chronicles 29:17)

Jesus said, "I am the Way, the Truth, and the Life. No one comes to the Father except through me." God wants us to discover Him, and experience Him through personal relationship and one-on-one encounter with Him. He wants us to know that we can trust Him. Do you trust Him today? Will you give Him a chance in your life—your heart?

"Let not the wise man glory in his wisdom, let not the mighty man glory in his might, nor let the rich man glory in his riches; but let him who glories glory in this—that he understands and knows Me, that I am the LORD, exercising loving kindness, judgment, and righteousness in the earth. For in these I delight." (Jeremiah 9:23-24)

We should desire to come into a greater understanding of the goodness of God and the Gospel of Jesus Christ. "For it is God who commanded light to shine out of darkness, who has shown in our hearts to give the light of the knowledge of the glory of God in the face of Jesus Christ" The fact that we call ourselves Christians, Saints of God, Ministers of the Gospel, etc., infers that we desire to dwell in the presence of the Lord living in oneness with Him, fulfilling our purpose in Him and exercising the authority He has given us through the Holy Spirit.

"For the earth will be filled with the knowledge of the glory of the LORD, as the waters cover the sea." (Habakkuk 2:14)

He has also given us assurance that, no matter how bad the situation may be, no one and nothing shall be able to destroy or uproot us, because we are in Him, just as He and the Father are one:

"I give them eternal life, and they shall never perish; no one will snatch them out of my hand. My Father, who has given

them to me, is greater than all; no one can snatch them out of my Father's hand. I and the Father are one." (John 10:28-30)

"I pray also for those who will believe in me through their message, that all of them may be one, Father, just as you are in me and I am in you. May they also be in us so that the world may believe that you have sent me. I have given them the glory that you gave me, that they may be one as we are one – I in them and you in me – so that they may be brought to complete unity" (John 17:20-23)

Through Prayer...

The word of God in Philippians 4:6 urges us to be careful for nothing; but in everything by prayer and supplication with thanksgiving, let our requests be made known to God.

Remember this one key point in praying, it is that God responds to your faith; another is, you must believe with all your heart and ask in Jesus' name. Faith being the operative word, *"let him ask in faith, nothing wavering,"* (James 1:5).

Pray without ceasing because prayer is a weapon of spiritual warfare and deliverance; also, for miracles and breakthrough. Faith moves God's heart and hand to act on your behalf. Instead of praying silently, speak into the air to destroy the satanic authority and establish the word of God prophetically. Satan is 'the prince of the power of the air,' as stated in the Bible in Ephesians 2:2.

So by releasing the prophetic words of Christ, you are speaking things into existence naturally that have already been established in the realm of the spirit.

When going to pray, you must prepare yourself to focus only on God and not think about your job, children, spouse, or what happened yesterday or this morning. When Jesus prayed, He went to a quiet place alone, and before daybreak, He prayed, sometimes day and night, He prayed. It is the place where you should be humble but in boldness make your supplication known. (A source once states, "Prayer is the place of admitting our need of desiring God to be our all in all, claiming dependence upon God." Some other definition sources say, "Becoming one with God and declaring His words," "exercising faith and hope," "the privilege of touching the heart of the Father through the Son of God, Jesus our LORD," and "A solemn request for help or expression of thanks addressed to God.")

From the beginning of time, man began to call upon the name of the Lord. Genesis 4:26 reminds us of this. Make it a habit to call on the Lord, and create a personal relationship with Him. As your relationship deepens, He will demonstrate His power in your life not just in this current generation but for generations to come. But we have to know Him and reflect His person so that our future generation will be open to Him as well. King David, a true servant of God, said this to his son, *"As for you, my son Solomon, know the God of your father, and serve Him with a loyal heart and with a willing mind; for the LORD searches all hearts and understands all the intent of the thoughts. If you seek Him, He will be found by you; but if you forsake Him, He will cast you off forever"* (1 Chronicles 28:9).

Looking at the example of Jesus Himself, the Bible tells of many instances where He prayed. He did so to ensure that He was in constant communion with God in order to carry out His will.

Through the Word of God...

After Jesus was baptized, He was led into the wilderness to be tempted by the devil (Matt 4:1-11). One of the tactics that Jesus used was speaking out the word of God, saying authoritatively, *"Do not put the LORD your God to the test. Worship the LORD your God, and serve Him only."* The scripture served as a sword to defeat the devil at that instance, for the word of God is alive and active, sharper than any double-edged sword, it penetrates even to dividing soul and spirit, joints and marrow; it judges the thoughts and attitudes of the heart (Heb. 4:12). Every word of God is pure. It is a shield unto those that put their trust in Him.

Furthermore, as it is written, "All scripture is given by inspiration of God, and is profitable for doctrine, for reproof, for correction, and for instruction in righteousness." This means that the Scripture — the Bible — tells us who we are as people of God, how we are to live, how to overcome the wiles of the devil and how to get close to God. Most importantly, it tells us of the promises God has for us.

"For I know the plans I have for you," declares the LORD, "plans to prosper you and not to harm you, plans to give you hope and a future" (Jeremiah 29:11)

In addition, your words should take their source from God's word in your daily interaction with people. In fact, the Bible likens our words to arrows. Luke 10:27 commands us to love the Lord our God with all our heart, with all our soul, with all our strength, with our entire mind, and our neighbor as ourselves. We are to encourage one another daily, so that none of us may be hardened by sin's deceitfulness. Remember that there is a judge for the one who rejects God and does not accept His words; and that every evil or bad word spoken will condemn that person at the last day.

Christ was appointed by God. *"Behold my servant, whom I have chosen"* (Matt.12:18). As a believer, you too have been appointed for the work of the Kingdom of God, which is to rescue nonbelievers from their kingdom of self. You're God's priest, called to invoke the power of the Word; you're His mouthpiece, created to declare and establish His will on earth. Prayer and the Word are your key tools to executing this assignment. You're a custodian of the Word because you are born of the Word. I say these things for you to check yourselves saints of God. We know the words of the Lord and so we need to apply it.

When God is pleased with what you are doing, you also experience His presence and power in your evangelistic efforts. Jesus overcame the trials God predicted He would face. You must not let anyone or anything get in the way of the fulfillment of the mission to take the gospel to people who have not heard; you must do this in spite of discouragement. Despite all challenges, overwhelming victory is ours through Christ, who loves us. Jesus said, "I am leaving you with a gift—peace of mind and heart. And the peace I give is a gift the world cannot give." So don't be troubled or afraid, but rather read and pray His word. His Word is the revelation you need to be and do all He has promised to you in the Scripture.

Your work for the kingdom of Christ depends upon the power and your knowledge of the Lord Jesus who lives and works in and through you. Apostle Paul stated *"He who has set me apart before I was born, and who called me by his grace, was pleased to reveal his Son to me, in order that I might preach Him among the Gentiles"* (Galations1:15). He goes on to say in Galatians 2:20, *"And the life I now live in the flesh I live by faith in the Son of God, who loved me, and gave himself for me."* How about being sold out to the Lord in that way? Well, spend time on your knees to accomplish more and study God's word on a daily basis, to learn from it, and to grow in it.

The need for prayer and studying the word in the life of a Christian worker is a necessity. When we are humble and follow the examples of the Bible, the Lord will add to the number day by day those who are being saved. We cannot exist by only what we see but by what God has told us to do.

How do we do this? Start by studying the words of God and praying them back to Him. The words of the Lord are gleaned precept upon precept, line upon line, here a little, there a little, and eventually break forth into an overflowing grace. All power has been given unto us through the Holy Spirit, and the Lord's blood that was shed, and in Him, we have the victory. As you surrender to Him, through the Word, the Holy Spirit, acting upon your will, over time, will help you develop your own style of fellowship with Heaven.

The word of God is a lamp unto our feet and a light unto our way. It is a mirror to our soul, a cleansing agent and food to our spirit. We were made in the image and likeness of God. As living stones, we are being built into a spiritual house to be a Holy Priesthood. We are a chosen people, a Royal Priesthood, a Holy Nation, God's special possession, so we must declare the praises of Him who called us out of darkness into his wonderful light. How would we know and pray this if we do not read the Word?

If you believe in the word of God, then you must believe everything that the Bible speaks of, not just some of the things. The word of God came from God's own mouth and it shall not return unto Him void, but it shall accomplish its purpose, and it shall prosper in the thing whereto He sent it. God sent His word and told us that His word is to remain in us; God's words are His character, the revelation of who He is and what His will is; and the promises of what He has for us.

The Bible tells us that if we live righteously and abide in His word, we will be like a tree planted by streams of water, which yields its fruits in season, whose leaves would never wither and whatever we do shall prosper.

Keep this Book of the Law always on your lips; meditate on it day and night, so that you may be careful to do everything written in it. Then you will be prosperous and successful. (Joshua 1:8)

Through Holy Living...

"As He who called you is holy, you also be holy in all your conduct, since it is written, and 'You shall be holy, for I am holy'" (1 Pet. 1:15–16).

The Bible speaks of such wonderful things such as the atonement (covering) and prayers of Christ (our chief intercessor) and also the Holy Spirit who intercedes on our behalf. This means that holiness must become visible in your life's journey.

Consider the narrative about the Samaritan woman at the well. As Jesus and her talked about their views on worship, the woman voiced her faith that the Messiah was coming and Jesus answered, *"I who speak to you am He."* (John 4:26). While the woman began to grasp the reality of her encounter with Jesus, the disciples returned and were shocked to find Him speaking to a woman.

However, Jesus moved her in such a way that she left behind her water jar and returned to the town, inviting the people to *"Come, see a man who told me all that I ever did"* (John 4:29). You see, sometimes God makes His way known to us but because of our own concerns, we miss Him. He already knows your past, but He also knows that He can set you free, if you allow Him. The right thing to do is, be humble and as children, receive Him and oh the joy we experience! We cannot help but make Him known to others.

When you build a personal relationship with Jesus, you become filled with the Holy Spirit. The Holy Spirit works as the motivating force in your life to propel you forward in spiritual purity. That Samaritan woman was filthy and dirty, but Jesus' words served as the living water of cleansing to her, for she was touched by Grace. The work of the Holy Spirit cannot happen unless we become born again: confess, repent and receive the forgiveness of our sins. Letting your sinful nature control your mind leads to death, but letting the Spirit control your mind leads to life and peace.

I recall an article I read once that said something like this, 'Anything that springs from self, however small it may be is sin. Self-complacency in service is sin. Self-seeking in business or Christian work is sin, touchiness, resentment worry, fear, all spring from self and all are sin and make our cups unclean." Behaviors such as those are ungodly and generate from a bad spirit; I can attest to that. Do we want our cups to be unclean? As for me, I want my cup to be filled with all of God's riches in glory and overflow. You're not alone; that

Samaritan woman had her own issues, but Jesus' words impacted and changed her forever.

Today, I want you to begin to grasp and do the same thing. We must not open doors that lead us to indulging in sin; this is the way we become bound with demonic chains. Things end up going the wrong way in our lives.

Let Jesus purify you daily. How would He do that? Through His words. *"Now you are clean through the words I have spoken to you,"* says Jesus. God wants us to be Christlike and so holy living is imperative, but we need the Holy Spirit to put the Word into effect in us. You too can be cleansed and changed like that woman, no matter how filthy you may be. His blood, His Word, His Spirit — that's all it takes.

Through Spiritual Authority...

Once you are born-again, for you to effectively operate from the baptism in the Holy Spirit and gifts of the

Holy Spirit, you must know who you are in Christ. Jesus said in John 14:12, *"Most assuredly I say unto you he who believes in me, the works that I do he will do also and greater works than these he will do because I go to my father."* Let it be according to your faith.

"I will give you the keys to the Kingdom of Heaven, and whatever you bind on earth will be bound in Heaven and whatever you loose on earth will be loosed in Heaven." (Matthew 16:19)

You will also declare a thing and it will be established for you, so light will shine on your ways. (Job 22:28).

"Nevertheless we made our prayer unto our God, and set a watch against them day and night, because of them" (Nehemiah 4:9)

Jesus Himself says that He has given us the authority to trample on serpents and scorpions and over all the power of the enemy, and nothing shall by any means hurt us (Luke 10:17), and to possess the Kingdom of

God on the earth by force (Matthew 11:12). We are his battle ax and weapons of war and with His own, He will break the nations in pieces and will destroy kingdoms, specifically the kingdom of Satan and of man. In other words, when situations challenge you, take authority, take it to the Lord in prayer and use the weapons that He has given you. (You will find out more about these later on in this book.)

"And whatever you ask in my name, that will I do, that the Father may be glorified in the Son. If you ask me anything in my name, I will do it." (John 14:13-14)

As Saints of God, we must remember that we have authority in the name of Jesus to be delivered from sin. The Bibles tells us that sin shall no longer be our master, because we are not under the law, but under grace. The law was brought in so that the trespass might increase. *"But where sin increased, grace increased all the more, so that just as sin reigned in death, so also grace might reign through righteousness to bring eternal life through Jesus Christ our Lord"* (Romans 5:??).

Spiritual authority goes hand in hand with spiritual purity. God wants us to be free from sin so power can freely flow in and through us. Holiness is a shield in warfare; it is the backbone of our spiritual authority. So pursuing holy living and a life of prayer develops a close relationship where you are protected by Christ.

You will not forget that you must reflect Him in all you say and do. The Lord says to, 'Be still, and know that I am God; I will be exalted among the nations, I will be exalted in the earth!' He wants to showcase His power and you're His means to doing that on earth. Jesus said that anyone who has faith in Him will do what He did and will do even greater things than that.

One sure sign of this walk with Jesus is the "peace" in your heart. His peace is not the absence of trials and tribulations, but an assurance that He's with you in the midst of all. Proverbs 16: 7 says: When a man's ways please the Lord, He makes even his enemies to be at peace with him. Therefore, since we have been made right in God's sight by faith, we have peace with God because of what Jesus Christ our Lord has done for us.

That inner peace strengthens you and makes you bold enough to demonstrate that spiritual authority He has given you.

Saints of God, the Lord is worthy to be praised. He and He alone gives His people strength and bless them with peace; self has no place in it.

Through Fellowship...

The church is referred to as the body of Christ, made up of many parts, but all working together for a common goal, which is mutual growth.

In many instances, Jesus reveals Himself to us through our fellowshipping together. Since Scripture says we know in part, then no person can survive on their own. We must receive from one another.

If you don't fellowship with others, if you don't belong to a local church where sound Bible doctrines are taught, you don't know Jesus; you haven't discerned the body of Christ. If you don't love your neighbor, you don't know God and you haven't seen Him; there is no proof of an encounter with Him.

The Bible tells us to not forsake the gathering—fellowship with the brethren—as is the habit of some, but encouraging one another even more as you see the day of the Lord coming nearer (Hebrews 10:25).

"Whoever says he is in the light and hates his brother is still in darkness; whoever loves his brother abides in the light" (1 John 2:9-10).

"And they continued steadfastly in the apostles' doctrine and fellowship, and in breaking of bread, and in prayers." (Acts 2:42)

Like the Early Church, we too must fellowship together. Our spiritual growth will be slow and erratic if we do not fellowship with other Christians who can share with us the revelation of Scripture.

Through Praise and Adoration...

Once we have the afore-mentioned principles in place, we can then live a life of sacrificial praise unto God by giving Him all the praise, honor and glory He deserves. We should take joy in knowing that the Lord inhabits the praises of His people.

He is:

Our Creator	Our Rock
Our Salvation	Our Provider
Our Peace	Our Righteousness
Our Healer	Our Banner
Our Shepherd	The Bread of Life
Our Deliverer	Consuming Fire
The Potter	The Light
The Way	The Truth
The Word	Our Teacher
Our Soul Savior	Our Soul Lover

The One that teaches our hands to war and our fingers
to fight
The One Who Is With Us

To Him be all the Glory!

It is a fact that only the Lord Himself can manifest all of
these characteristics due to His divine nature. Go ahead
shout Hallelujah, make a joyful noise unto him! If we
live a continuous life of praise and worship, we keep
His attention. Because He is the all-seeing and all-
knowing God, whatever we need to be done, He takes
care of it. Even the plans, plots and ploys of the enemy
are destroyed when we praise. God is mighty, and
having all the power, He knows our future and only
wants the best for us; this we are sure of. Elijah was a
human being, even as we are. He prayed earnestly that
it would not rain, and it did not rain on the land for
three and a half years (James 5:17); he revered the Lord.

"Sing for joy, O heavens, for the LORD has done this; shout aloud, O earth beneath. Burst into song, you mountains, you forests and all your trees." (Isaiah 44:23)

Saints of God, we need to constantly praise and be sure that His power is real. King Solomon asked for wisdom and received it and more; Nehemiah prayed for the restoration of Jerusalem and was granted favor and protection to accomplish His work. The disciples on the Day of Pentecost received the infilling of the Holy Spirit — and there many other stories. What was some of the things common with them all?

They prayed.

God remained faithful to them.

They trusted in God solely and prayed knowing that only God could help them.

They all fulfilled the purpose that God had for them.

These stories are not for us to read for entertainment and say praise God. They were written as a guideline as to what we should do. Remember, God knows the plans that He has for us and once we are in His will, praying His words back to Him, we will accomplish what has been set for us to do. As spiritual beings, this is our spiritual act of worship. So offer your body as a living sacrifice to God by being holy (set apart, sacred) which pleases God. God is not a respecter of persons, neither does He show favoritism; we are just like the people of old and we serve the same God.

Others will then want to taste and see that the LORD is God.

"And at midnight Paul and Silas prayed, and sang praises to God: and the prisoners heard them." (Acts 16:25)

In this particular situation after Paul and Silas were beaten, chained and imprisoned, instead of fretting, they prayed and sang hymns to God. In doing so, there was a violent earthquake that shook the prison, thereby opening all the prison doors and loosening the chains of all the prisoners. The prison guard who was amazed that the prisoners had not escaped accepted Christ as his Savior and all of his family got baptized.

Through Worship: Fasting, Tithing & Service...

We also worship him for things to come as well. The things that we need to lead a successful life in Christ have been in existence from the beginning of time. So as His words declare, we just have to walk in them. What things you may ask; dominion and authority in Christ, praying His words, hearing from Him, and being directed by Him. People will see the glory of the LORD surrounding you as God gives you joy. Yes, He makes us happy! For you will never be lacking in zeal, but keep your spiritual fervor, serving the LORD. It is the LORD God we must follow, and Him we must revere. We must keep His commands and obey Him; serve Him and hold fast to Him. We were called to be free but not to use our freedom to indulge in sinful nature but serve one another in love.

We should use whatever gifts we have received to serve others; faithfully administering God's grace in its various forms just as Jesus demonstrated. The Son of Man did not come to be served, but to serve, and to give His life as a ransom for us. No one can serve two masters; either he will hate the one and love the other or he will be devoted to the one and despise the other. You cannot serve both God and Mammon (material things or self). Either we are serving the LORD doing His will or we are not.

A life of worship and service to God and His people is pleasing to Him. A life of love is a life of impact, a blessing to others, and a reflector of God's kind nature.

Furthermore, we must devote ourselves to fasting. Dwell in His presence, fast, pray and pay tithes. Apostle Paul said that he kept his body under subjection so that when he preached, he too will not be cast away (1 Corinthians 9:27). Once we stay prayed up filling up our spirit with the word of God, we ultimately have to live what he has commanded us to do. When Esther and her people fasted and prayed, Haram was destroyed for trying to destroy God's people. What Haman built for Mordecai, he reaped it. All of God's servants did it, Nehemiah, Joel, David and the list goes on.

"And I set my face unto the Lord God, to seek by prayer and supplications, with fasting, and sackcloth, and ashes." (Daniel 9:3)

Why should we worship God? He is the supplier of all substance and a right way for us and our children. We are blessed when we hunger and thirst after righteousness — for the Lord fills us. Saints of God, when we seek the Lord in fasting, He looses the bands of wickedness. He undoes the heavy burdens. He lets the oppressed go free. He breaks every yoke. Again, we grow to know the Helper, who is the Holy Spirit, whom the Father sent in Jesus' name to teach us all things and bring to our memory all Jesus said.

I most of all love the fact that we become separated (set apart) do the work we are called to do! So then do not be surprised if your family, friends, co-workers etc., become hostile and or distance themselves from you, or even if you find yourself face to face in a physical battle with them. Stand up and show that you know who God is and that His Spirit works in you.

"You make known to me the path of life; in your presence there is fullness of joy; at your right hand are pleasures forevermore." (Psalms 16:11)

There are not enough words to describe the power and person of the Almighty, the King of Glory! We were made in His image and likeness; created beings, created by Him who was, and is and, is to come. God sent His Son to die for all of our sins, who rose from the dead three days after that so that those believing in Him should not perish but have everlasting life. He is a God who offers protection when we keep our end of the bargain and give our 10 percent—tithes—back to Him. Have you ever wondered why it is so easy for some of us to go out to restaurants and dine paying gratuities of 15 percent or more, yet we cannot give our God 10 percent?

"Bring ye all the tithes into the storehouse, that there may be meat in mine house, and prove me now herewith, saith the Lord of hosts, if I will not open you the windows of heaven, and pour you out a blessing, that there shall not be room enough to receive it. And I will rebuke the devourer for your sakes, and he shall not destroy the fruits of your ground; neither shall your vine cast her fruit before the time in the field, saith the Lord of hosts. And all nations shall call you blessed: for ye shall be a delightsome land, saith the Lord of hosts." (Malachi 3:10-12).

Through Thanksgiving...

Another key factor is to say thank you to the LORD for everything. As you go about your daily life, try it before you perform each action and see the difference in your life. In Luke 1:47-49, Mary the mother of Jesus said, "My spirit rejoices in God, my Savior, for He has looked on the humble estate of his servant. For behold, from now on all generations will call me blessed; for He who is mighty has done great things for me, and holy is his name." You must express gratitude, how much you love Him. Even though you do not see Him now, you must show how much you believe in Him and are filled with an inexpressible and glorious joy towards Him. There will be the crown of righteousness laid up for you which the LORD, the righteous judge, will award to you.

I tell you the truth saints of God; He gives power to the weak and strength to the powerless. The Bible declares that even youths will become weak and tired, and young men will fall in exhaustion; but those who trust in the LORD will find new strength. Shouldn't we thank Him for giving us strength to scale through those things that could otherwise have made us weak, weary, and fall?

When we give thanks, He is faithful to pour out all of His promises.

"Bless the Lord oh my soul and all that is within me bless His holy name." (Psalm 103:1)

When we worship our faithful and holy Creator, those who are humble shall hear of Him and rejoice with us. The promises of God are all yes and through Him, they are all Amen.

"He raises the poor from the dust and lifts the needy from the ash heap; He seats them with princes and has them inherit a throne of honor." (I Samuel 2:8)

When we bless His name and give Him thanks, He becomes happy. That is why the commandment says, "Thou should not use the LORD's name in vain, for the LORD will not hold you guiltless who misuse his name."

So we should see the importance of communing regularly with God and should now understand why we should pray and pray His word. I believe that when we pray God's words back to Him, it calls forth what God has already purposed and predestined.

Through writing this book, it is my hope that the word of God, which is living and active transforms your life and starts to work within you now. I hope that you see God's character revealed in its fullness and believe in him even more.

Walk into your fullness in God with holy faith and realize that there is no separation in Christ and we are all one. Watch the word of the LORD work like a consuming fire in your life, 'like a hammer that breaks rocks into pieces?'

III

PRAYING THE OUR FATHER PRAYER

Remember that the devil who is the 'prince of the power of the air' is on an all-out attack to kill, destroy and steal from us so that we fall out of alignment or never come into our full purpose in God. So spiritual attack will come in various ways to our life, our families, and our faith, finances, etc. You can overcome this war by using the weapons that the word of the LORD has given us. With the words of the LORD being the sword of the spirit, approach the throne of God boldly.

Here are some ways we can invoke God's power in our daily contention with temptations, and the enemy:

The Sword of the Spirit — The word of God which you are now applying to your everyday life
The Blood of Jesus — His blood purges, remits sin, redeems, heals, delivers and sets free
Marching/walking/stomping/dancing/clapping — The Lord inhabits our worship

Silence — It is good to wait quietly for the salvation of the LORD.

Shouting — Shouting brought down the walls of Jericho.

Tithes/Offerings — It opens the windows of Heaven and brings blessings.

God's ability can be accessed through His names too. Use the names of God; whatever name you call Him, that is what He becomes and manifests to you. Here are a few:

Adonai (Lord, Master)

El Elyon (The Most High God)

El Olam (The Everlasting God)

El Shaddai (Lord God Almighty)

Elohim (God)

Jehovah Jireh (The Lord Will Provide)

Jehovah Maccadeshem (The Lord Who Sanctifies)

Jehovah Nissi (The Lord My Banner)

Jehovah Rapha (The Lord That Heals)

Jehovah Sabaoth (The Lord of Hosts)

Jehovah Shalom (The Lord Is Peace)

Jehovah Tsidkenu (The Lord Our Righteousness)

Jehovah-Raah (The Lord My Shepherd)

Yahweh (Lord, Jehovah)

THE OUR FATHER PRAYER...

Our Father Who Art in Heaven

Establish your covenant relationship with God as your father. He is your daddy who you represent. A father is a "source;" from the Greek word "ABBA." He should be your one and only source. He is also father to everyone who acknowledges Him. Jesus said, *"My Father's house has many rooms; if that were not so, I would have told you that. I am going there to prepare a place for you?"* Pray not only for yourself but also for others. Remember that the Bible admonishes us to bear one another's burdens to fulfill the law of Christ. Call out the names of your family, loved ones and others as the Spirit leads.

Let us pray…

I will praise you oh LORD! for I am fearfully and wonderfully made. Marvelous are your works, and my soul knows very well. You are my LORD Maccadeshem and the one who formed me in my mother's womb.

Hallelujah! We give you praise, for we are your workmanship, created in Christ Jesus for good works, which you have prepared beforehand that we should walk in them.

Amazing are your plans for us dear LORD. We know what they are, as your word declares; plans to prosper us and not to harm us, plans to give us hope and a future. Praises be to your name, Hallelujah! The gifts and the calling of God are irrevocable! And you are able to make all (not just some) grace abound toward us. That we, always having all capability in all things, may flourish in every good work. For this we give you praise!

Surely, LORD, You bless the righteous; you surround them with your favor as with a shield. LORD, you will be our dwelling place in all generations. You are good! I am poor and you raise me up from the dust and lifted me; who have been in need from the ash heap, to make me sit with Princes and inherit a seat of honor. LORD, I thank You, LORD I love you. You are my all in all and all I need. They that dwell in the secret place of the most high shall abide in the shadow of El Shaddai.

We thank and praise You, O God of our fathers: you have given us wisdom and power. Oh, the depth of the riches of the wisdom and knowledge of you! How unsearchable are your judgments, and your paths beyond tracing out!

Adonai to that man who pleases you, you give wisdom, knowledge and happiness, but to the sinners you give the task of gathering and storing up wealth to hand it over to the one who pleases you! It is the spirit in a man, the breath of the Almighty that gives understanding.

Teach us wisdom in the innermost place Almighty God, just as you gave to those four young men: knowledge and understanding of all kinds of literature and learning. For wisdom is more precious than rubies, and nothing we desire can compare with her.

Then, your peace, Shalom, which is beyond our utmost understanding, will keep and guard our hearts and thoughts, in Christ Jesus.

Change our times and seasons, according to your will oh LORD, just as you set up kings and depose them. Give wisdom to the wise and knowledge to the discerning.

By your wisdom, you laid the earth's foundations, by your understanding, you set the heavens in place; and by your knowledge, the deeps were divided.

Put your law in our minds and write it on our hearts, you are our Jehovah Jireh!

We will trust in you LORD with all my heart, and lean not on our own understanding; in all our ways, we will acknowledge you, and you shall direct our paths in Jesus' name. Amen.

Hallowed Be Thy Name!

Respect the name of the LORD, He has all the power. He is reverenced, set apart, sanctified, El Elyon. Magnify God for all of His attributes; He is King, faithful God, ever-loving Savior, provider, dependable Lord, our very present help, a shelter in the time of storm, Jehovah Nissi. Only a divine heavenly Father can be all of these characteristics and more. Psalms 20:7 says, "Some trust in chariots and some trust in horses, but we trust in the name of the LORD our God!"

Let us pray...

Jehovah Nisi, who among the gods is like you? You are majestic in holiness, awesome in glory, and working wonders. I admonish everyone and everything on earth to worship you in the splendor of Your Holiness. I bow down in worship; kneel before you, for you are my maker.

El Shaddai, you deserve the honor, glory and the praise! Let us be separated from our flesh and be devoted like the angels who stand around the throne, elders and four living creatures, falling down on their faces worshiping you. So we can be holy as your word speaks of holiness — holy ground, holy assemblies, a holy nation, holy garments, a holy city, holy promises, holy men and women, Holy Scriptures, holy hands and a holy faith.

LORD Jesus, you are highly exalted, you stretch out your right hand, and the earth swallows your enemies. Your statutes stand firm; holiness adorns your house for endless days. Your love is unfailing and your strength guides your people to your holy dwelling.

Holy, Holy, Holy is the LORD Almighty! Elohim, the whole earth is full of your glory. You reign forever and ever.

Jesus, you are the true and living God and our everlasting King! Take joy in what you hear and be pleased with our worship. El Roi, let it be a sweet smelling aroma unto you. To you LORD who is holy and true, all power and glory is given. For it is you who opens doors no one can shut, and who shuts doors that no one can open.

Lord God, we know also that it is you who have given us understanding, so that we may know Him who is true. How marvelous are your grace and mercy towards us! For your word said that if we consent and obey, we will eat the best of the land. You will not let our foot slip, for you who watches over us, will not slumber nor sleep.

God, you are not a man that you should lie, or repent. What you say we believe that you will do. You will destroy the wisdom of the wise, and the cleverness of the clever you will set aside.

For as many as are the promises of God, in you they are yes! Also through you is our Amen to the glory of God. You have sealed us and given us the Spirit in our hearts as a pledge. And if we are faithless, you remain faithful, for you cannot deny yourself. And so Holy Father we praise you, for those who suffer according to your will shall entrust their souls to a faithful Creator in doing what is right. LORD, we trust you in the name of Jesus.

Yahveh Tzidkenu, you are righteous in all your ways and loving toward all you have created. Let us blow the trumpets and sound the alarm. Your way is perfect, flawless and you are a shield for all who take refuge in you. Lord, you are exalted in power; in you justice and great righteousness exist, and we give thanks and praise because you do not oppress.

For I know that you search minds and hearts of men, bring to an end the violence of the wicked, and make the righteous secure by being a righteous judge, who expresses your wrath every day. Oh LORD, yet you have put me on the path of life and have filled me with joy in your presence!

You are righteous, O LORD, your laws are right. Let us be exalted by your justice, so that you can continue to show yourself holy and know that anyone who boasts should boast in you and understand and know that you are the LORD, who exercises kindness, justice and righteousness on earth. For it is in those things you take delight.

Your righteousness is like the mighty mountains, your justice like the great deep. O LORD, you preserve both man and beast. Oh, how we praise and love you Almighty and righteous one. We sing praises to your name forever. Be pleased with our worship oh LORD, may your presence, your power, your spirit be always here with us in Jesus' name. Amen.

Your Kingdom Come, Your Will Be Done On Earth As It Is In Heaven

A kingdom is a system governed by a king where the king rules over a territory (land, systems, institutions and people etc.). The Kingdom of God is spiritual. The LORD intended for man to have dominion and rule over the earth, taking up his rightful authority as kings and priests. The Kingdom of God is in you and me, which is righteousness, peace and joy in the Holy Spirit. This comes from within us, being spiritual beings. That is why the Bible tells us not to be conformed to the patterns of this world, but be transformed by the renewing of the mind. Then you will be able to test and approve what God's will is — His good, pleasing and perfect will (Romans 12:2). By praying that the Kingdom of God should come on earth, you will be praying for others and yourself to be healed from sickness, free from bondage and strongholds. Like the LORD, you will be gracious and compassionate, slow to anger and rich in love.

Seek the Kingdom of God first.
Let us pray…

LORD, you perform wonders that cannot be fathomed, miracles that cannot be counted. How many are your works, LORD! In wisdom you made them. All the earth is full of your creations.

No one can probe the limits of the Almighty. How great are your works, Oh LORD, how profound are your thoughts! Great is the LORD and most worthy of praise!

Ah, Sovereign LORD, you have made the heavens and the earth by your great power and outstretched arm.

Nothing is too hard for you. Nothing in all creation is hidden from your sight. Everything is uncovered and lay bare before your eyes; to which we must give account. Oh LORD, I know so well that with man, this is impossible, but with you, all things are possible.

Every good and perfect gift is from above. Coming down from my Father of the heavenly lights, who does not change like shifting shadows. He remains the same, and His years will never end.

Great is my LORD, mighty in power; His understanding has no limit. Ah, yes my LORD for I know that you are the one who is able to do exceeding abundantly above all that we ask or think, according to the power that works in us!

To the only God my Savior be glory, majesty, power and authority in Jesus' name. Let us praise the name of the LORD: for His name alone is excellent; His glory is above the earth and heaven. Your Kingdom shall reign over all the earth. From Jesus Christ, who is the faithful witness, and the prince of the kings of the earth. That loved us, and washed us from our sins in His own blood, and has made us kings and priests to God and His Father; to Him be glory and dominion forever and ever.

He was given authority, glory and sovereign power; all nations and peoples of every language worshiped Him. His dominion is an everlasting dominion that will not pass away, and His kingdom is one that will never be destroyed. For yours is the kingdom, the power and the Glory in Jesus' name. Amen.

You are called of God for a significant work in His Kingdom, if you submit to Him. If you prepare to do the LORD's good work, no weapon formed against you shall prosper. Ephesians 2:10 assures us that we are God's workmanship, created in Christ Jesus to do good works, which God prepared in advance for us. That work is to proclaim good news to the poor, bind up the brokenhearted, and proclaim freedom for the captives and release from darkness for the prisoners. All authority has been given to Jesus Christ who commanded us to go into the entire world and teach all nations. He has given us the keys to the Kingdom.

Give Us Today Our Daily Bread

Philippians 4:19 declares that God will meet all our needs according to His riches in glory. I must emphasize that you are not just to pray to have the Lord supply your needs but also the needs of others such as your family members, community, government, country, and the nations.

Let us pray...

Oh God my father, you are my Jehovah Jireh, I shall not want for anything!

LORD, you have poured out your Spirit upon me and your law is perfect, reviving the soul. I thank you that we are a chosen people, a royal priesthood, a holy nation, God's special possession; that we may declare the praises of Him who called us out of darkness into His wonderful light. If we obey you fully and keep your covenant, then out of all nations, we will be your treasured possession. The people walking in darkness have seen a great light; on those living in the land of deep darkness, a light has dawned.

You give water in the wilderness, rivers in the desert, to give drink to your chosen people, the people whom you formed for yourself that they might declare your praise! Adonai, continue to activate your Spirit within us, that we may live. For if we live according to the flesh, we will die, but if by the Spirit we put to death the deeds of the body, we shall live. How much more will you our heavenly Father give the Holy Spirit to those who ask you! For the Helper (the Holy Spirit) will teach me all things and bring to my memory all that Christ has said to me and give me peace. Your love has been poured in my heart according to the riches of your glory. My heart will not be troubled but I will receive power when the Holy Spirit has come upon me. He is my gift. We will possess the fruit of the Spirit which is love, joy, peace, patience, kindness, goodness, faithfulness, gentleness, self-control; against such things, there is no law. I know that I live in you and you in me because you have given me of your Spirit. You LORD also will be a refuge for the oppressed, a refuge in times of trouble.

Father, I believe in the LORD Jesus Christ, save me and my household. Your word said that if I pay attention to the laws and I'm careful to follow them, then you will keep your covenant of love with me. LORD, love me, bless me and increase my numbers. Bless the fruits of my womb, the crops of my land. Keep me free from every disease. I will not worry about my life; what I will eat or drink; or what I will wear. Christ said my life is worth more than food, and my body more than clothes. The birds of the air do not sow or reap or store away in barns, and yet my heavenly Father feeds them. You clothe the grass of the field. The flowers of the field grow and do not labor or spin and I am much more valuable than they. Worrying is useless to my purpose. For the pagans run after all these things, and my heavenly Father knows that I need them. I will seek first your Kingdom and righteousness, and all these things will be given to me. Hallelujah, all things work together for good to those who love the LORD. I am called according to your purpose.

El Elyon is with me, a mighty One who will save. You will rejoice over me with gladness; you will quiet me by your love. You will exult over me with loud singing. When my spirit faints within me, you know my way!

Oh yes, you love your people, all your holy ones are in your hand. If you are for us, who can be against us? You did not spare your own Son but gave Him up for us all. How will you not also with Him graciously give us all things?

When I thought my foot slipped off your steadfast love, O LORD, you held me up. When the cares of my heart are many, your consolations cheer my soul. Praises be on to your Name!

Oh what love you have given to me, that I should be called a child of God! You have multiplied, O LORD my God, your wondrous deeds and your thoughts toward me. None can compare with you! I will proclaim and tell of them, yet they are more than can be told.

For I am sure that neither death, nor life, nor angels, nor rulers, nor things present, nor things to come, nor powers, nor height, nor depth, nor anything else in all creation, will be able to separate me from the love of God in Christ Jesus.

I recognize that the LORD is the Spirit, and where the Spirit of the LORD is, there is freedom. LORD God, I thank you for freedom and prosperity in Jesus' name. Amen.

Side Note: Remember that God combines His name with the action that He is willing to perform. Jehovah Rophe, Jehovah Jireh, Jehovah Nissi, etc.

Forgive Us Our Debts As We Forgive Our Debtors

John 3:16-17 says for God so loved the world that He gave His only begotten son that whoever believes in Him should not perish but have ever lasting life. Blessed are the merciful for they will be shown mercy.

For God did not send His son into the world to condemn the world but to save the world through Him (John 3:17).

Let us pray…

Create in me a clean heart, Jehovah Gmolah, and renew a right, persevering, and steadfast spirit within me. Cast me not away from your presence and take not your Holy Spirit from me. Restore to me the joy of your salvation and uphold me with a willing spirit.

Though my sins are like scarlet, I ask that you let them be as white as snow. Though they are red as crimson, let them be like wool. Father God, though I am not worthy, behold my affliction and my pain and forgive all my depraved thinking and doing. Forgive my debts, and help me to forgive my debtors. For if I forgive people their trespasses, their reckless and willful sins, leaving them, letting them go, and giving up resentment, you will also forgive me.

For you, O LORD, are abundant in mercy and loving-kindness to all those who call upon you. Oh LORD my God, help me to not cover but forgive offenses as many as up to seventy times seven and seek love, instead of repeating a matter to separate even close friends.

Let me walk in the light, as Jesus is in the light, and have fellowship one with another. The blood of Jesus purifies me from all sin. If I confess my sins, you are faithful and just and will forgive me and purify me from all unrighteousness.

Your word says that if your people, who are called by your name, shall humble themselves, pray, seek, crave, and require of necessity your face and turn from their wicked ways, then will you forgive their sin, and heal their land, through Jesus Christ. LORD God, we have no power, only that which you have given us, by your Blood, your Spirit and your Word.

Cleanse me with hyssop, and I will be clean; oh LORD. Wash me, and I will be whiter than snow. Swept away my offenses like a cloud, my sins like the morning mist. I come to you LORD, for only you can redeem me. There have been those who came out of great tribulation who have washed their robes and made them white in the blood of the Lamb.

LORD Jesus, you are the way and the truth and the life. I forsake my wicked ways and evil thoughts and turn to you. Have mercy on me oh LORD and pardon me. To you be honor and might forever.

You gave yourself to redeem me from all wickedness, for me to gain access by faith into this grace. I rejoice in the hope of the glory of God. I believe in you!

My LORD and God, your word says that if we confess with our mouth and believe in our heart that Jesus was raised from the dead, we will be saved. May every knee bow and every tongue confess that Jesus Christ is Lord! For you are not slow in keeping your promises. You are patient not wanting anyone to perish, but everyone to come to repentance. It is a dreadful thing to fall into the hands of the living God, He is just and a righteous judge.

The revelation waits an appointed time; it speaks of the end and will not prove false. Though it lingers, I will wait for it; it will certainly come and will not delay.

There is only one lawgiver and judge, the One who is able to save and destroy. Rain on the righteous and the unrighteous. Once I was alienated from God and was an enemy in my mind because of my evil behavior.

But my God so loved the world that He gave His one and only Son, that whoever believes in Him shall not perish but have eternal life. Again you did not send your Son into the world to condemn the world, but to save the world.

Oh LORD, I thank you that through wisdom a house is built, by understanding, it is established; and by knowledge, the rooms shall be filled with all precious and pleasant riches. By your divine wisdom, help me to prepare my work outside and make it ready for the field. Your laws say that we shall not have in our bags differing weights, in our house differing measures but full and just weights; and a full and just measures.

LORD, allow me to be the one who deals generously and lends, and conducts my affairs with justice. Not as the poor man, he who works with a negligent hand, but to have a hand of the diligent to be rich. Woe to him who builds his house without righteousness and his upper rooms without justice.

74

LORD, your word says that he who is faithful in very little things is faithful also in much; and he who is unrighteous in very little things is unrighteous also in much. But godliness actually is a means of great gain when accompanied by contentment. Open for me your good storehouse, the heavens, give rain to my land and bless all the work of my hands. Oh mighty God, let me lend to many and not borrow. Free me from the spirit of offense: offending others and others offending me.

For I know too well that wealth obtained by fraud dwindles, but the one who gathers by labor increases it. Keep my life free from the love of money, so that I am content with what I have. Not withholding good from those to whom it is due, when it is in my power to do it and owing nothing to anyone except to love one another.

Likewise, my Lord and Savior, help me to be true in all things with my superiors who are in Christ, according to the flesh; not with eye service, as men pleasers; but in singleness of heart, fearing you while they do the same thing: giving up threatening, knowing that both their Master and mine is in heaven, and there is no partiality with you.

LORD, I will honor you from my wealth and from the first of all my produce plus more. LORD, I will fear not, for you have redeemed me, and have called me by my name. I am yours oh LORD. Oh how you love me! I love because you first loved me. God, you are love and whoever lives in love lives in you, and you in them. This is how love is made complete among us, so that we will have confidence on the Day of Judgment. Help us to be more like you.

Side Note: Un-forgiveness is a wall, a barrier that prevents the Holy Spirit from operating in you fully in the way He wants. If you are praying this prayer and the LORD shows you that someone has something against you or you have bitterness against someone, ask the LORD for His wisdom and leading to reconcile the situation. It is more dangerous for you to have bitterness against someone than if they have something against you. Bitterness open doors to evil spirits which bounds even Christians from living a wholesome life in God.

Moreover, the LORD Jesus Himself says that we should forgive others seventy times seven (in one day). That means for every time someone wrongs you, you must forgive. Your prayer will not be answered if you come before the LORD with a heart full of iniquity. People who conceal their sins will not prosper, but if they confess and turn from them, they will receive mercy (Proverbs 28:13). The LORD hates workers of iniquity.

Whoever walks in integrity will be delivered, but he who is crooked in his ways will suddenly fall. (Proverbs 28:18)

The arrogant cannot stand in your presence. You hate all who do wrong. (Psalms 5:5)

When a righteous person turns away from his righteousness and does injustice, he shall die for it; for the injustice that he has done he shall die (Ezekiel 18:26).

There are six things the LORD hates, seven that are detestable to him: haughty eyes, a lying tongue, hands that shed innocent blood, a heart that devises wicked schemes, feet that are quick to rush into evil, a false witness who pours out lies and a person who stirs up conflict in the community. Proverbs 6:16-19

Lead Us Not Into Temptation But Deliver Us From Evil

I Corinthians 10:13 says no temptation has seized you except what is common to man. This means that the temptation and struggles that you have or maybe faced with are not new. John 10:10 says. "The thief comes to kill, steal, and destroy: I have come that you may have life and have it more abundantly." This is the main reason for spiritual warfare and deliverance prayers.

Let us pray…

Lord Jesus, I do not fear, for you are with me; I am not dismayed, for you are my God who will strengthen and help me; and uphold me with your righteous right hand.

So I say with confidence, the Lord is my helper; I will not be afraid. What can mere mortals and the cares of this life do to me?

In times of sorrow, death, indecision and despair, you will keep me in perfect peace. My mind will be steadfast because I trust in you. Jehovah Shalom, you will not make me anxious about anything, but in every situation, by prayer and petition, and with thanksgiving, you will hear my request and your peace, which transcends all understanding, will guard my heart and my mind in Christ Jesus!

Your Holy Spirit is my helper. In the times of my weaknesses when I do not know what to pray for, He himself will intercede for me through wordless groans.

And I know that all things work for the good of those who love you, who have been called according to your purpose.

Blessed is the one who perseveres under trial and do not make light of the LORD's discipline. I will not lose heart when you rebuke me, because the LORD disciplines the one He loves, and He chastens everyone He accepts as His son.

Therefore, my feeble arms and weak knees will be strengthened. I will be careful that I do not fall. No temptation will overtake me. Lord, you will not put more on me than I can bear. You have prepared my hands to war and my fingers to fight and my body that I may run through troops and leap over walls.

Jehovah Rohi, by your divine power, you have given me everything I need for living a godly life. I declare receipt of it now from coming to know you. The one who has called me to yourself by means of your marvelous glory and excellence! Make my deserts like Eden.

Unleash your wrath into the hands of my tormentors, and let them release unto me all the wealth that belongs to me.

Jehovah Gibbor, contend, O LORD, with those who contend with me, fight against those who fight against me. Take up shield and buckler; arise and come to my aid. Brandish spear and javelin against those who pursue me. They make their tongues as sharp as a serpent's. The poison of vipers is on their lips. But your word is like fire, living and active and sharper than any double-edged sword. Penetrate even to divide their souls and spirits, joints and marrows. Overthrow their plans and let them be persecuted by the angels of the

LORD. Let them be confounded and put to shame, and brought to confusion as chaff driven by the wind.

Since they hid their net from me without cause and without cause dug a pit for me, may ruin overtake them by surprise. May the net they hid entangle them, may they fall into the pit, to their ruin. When I stumbled, they gathered in glee; assailants gathered against me without my knowledge. They slandered me without ceasing. Like the ungodly, they maliciously mocked and they gnashed their teeth at me.

In the name of Jesus. I come against and dismantle every word spoken contrary to your original plans and purposes for my destiny; every curse, witchcraft prayer, even plans and plots. Muzzle their mouths and numb their tongues. Though they use their actions, thoughts and deeds to destroy me; let the heavens bow down with divine judgment to scatter them. I will not lose my possessions due to their relentless desires for my destruction. For the weapons I fight with are not the weapons of the world but divine power to demolish strongholds. Lord Jesus, I pray that you confirm the word of your servant and fulfill the counsel of your messenger.

Release divine ambush on the camp of your enemies that surround me as you did with Balaam for you are the same yesterday, today and tomorrow. The devil will not have control over those who work with me, my family, my purpose and calling, neither will he be able to use them for evil. Not a word from their mouth will be wickedness, their heart will not be filled with malice and their throats will not be an open grave. For the devil is defeated and you are exalted. So let God and His Kingdom arise and let His enemies scatter.

I decree that your light has come into the world, but some people love darkness instead of light. Everyone who does evil hates the light, and will not come into the light for fear that their deeds will be exposed. But whoever lives by the truth comes into the light, so that it may be seen plainly that what they have done has been done in the sight of God.

I will not be afraid of those who kill the body because they cannot kill the soul.

But the cowardly, the unbelieving, the vile, the murderers, the sexually immoral, those who practice magic arts, the idolaters and all liars, they will be consigned to the fiery lake of burning sulfur and God Himself, our God is a Consuming Fire!

Gird your sword upon your side, O mighty One; clothe yourself with splendor and majesty. For you will grant that the enemies who rise up against me be defeated. They will come at me from one direction but flee from me in seven.

You prepare a table before me in the presence of my enemies. I'm persecuted, but not forsaken; cast down, but not destroyed. I am the head and not the tail. I'm a vessel full of power, knowledge, love and a sound mind from the Lord! I decree and declare that I am blessed in the city and in the field, going in and coming out. Greater is He that is within me than he that is in the world.

Lord Jesus, I thank you for being my Jehovah Shammah. I come against all backlash in your name and bind them up by your blood and your Holy Spirit in Jesus' name. Amen.

Side note: Remember what the Bible says about offences and forgiveness. Reflect on the entire passage from Matthew 18.

For Yours is the Kingdom, the Power and the Glory

What can we say about the Kingdom of God? The word of God has told us many things, especially from the mouth of Jesus Himself! But some will hear and understand while others will not get a clue. Jesus said,

"He that has ears let him hear." As for us, let us worship God in His entire splendor, because you are sure that the kingdom belongs to Him as well as all power and glory. The kingdom also refers to the world systems such as the education system, law, medical, healthcare, financial, etc. You are giving God thanks because you know that He has answered your prayers. When the righteous cry out to Him, he hears and answers, He will do just what He said He will do.

The kingdom of the world has become the kingdom of our Lord and of His Messiah, and He will reign forever and ever (Revelation 11:15).

Let us pray…

I decree and declare that the kingdom of heaven rules and reign. Jesus, you are the true and living God and our everlasting King! Take joy in what you hear and be pleased with our worship. El Roi, let it be a sweet smelling aroma unto you. To you LORD who is holy and true, all power and glory is given. For it is you who opens doors no one can shut, and who shuts doors that no one can open.

LORD Jesus, we know also that it is you who has given us understanding, so that we may know Him who is true. How marvelous are your grace and mercy towards us! For your word says that if we consent and obey, we will eat the best of the land. You will not let our foot slip for you who watches over us, will not slumber nor sleep.

God, you are not a man that you should lie or repent; what you say, we believe that you will do. You will destroy the wisdom of the wise, and the cleverness of the clever you will set aside.

For as many as are the promises of God, in you they are yes! Also through you is our Amen to the glory of God. You have sealed us and given us the Spirit in our hearts as a pledge. And if we are faithless, you remain faithful, for you cannot deny yourself.

And so Jesus we praise you, for those who suffer according to your will shall entrust their souls to a faithful Creator in doing what is right. Yahveh Tzidkenu, you are righteous in all your ways and loving toward all you have created. Let us blow the trumpets and sound the alarm. Your way is perfect, flawless and you are a shield for all who take refuge in you. Lord, you are exalted in power; in you justice and great righteousness exist, and we give thanks and praise because you do not oppress.

For I know that you search minds and hearts of men, bring to an end the violence of the wicked, and make the righteous secure by being a righteous judge, who expresses your wrath every day. Oh LORD, yet you have put me on the path of life and have filled me with joy in your presence, for your kingdom sake!

You are righteous, O LORD. My King, your laws are right. Let us be exalted by your justice, so that you can continue to show yourself holy and know that anyone who boasts should boast in you and understand and know that you are the LORD, who exercises kindness, justice and righteousness on earth. For it is in those things you take delight.

Your righteousness is like the mighty mountains, your justice like the great deep. Oh LORD, you preserve both man and beast. We praise and love you Almighty and righteous One. We sing praises to your name and adore you forever. Be pleased with our worship oh LORD, and may your presence, your power, your Spirit and Kingdom be always here with us and around us.

I thank and praise you, the God of my fathers. You have given me wisdom and power. Oh, the depth of the riches of the wisdom and knowledge of you! How unsearchable are your judgments, and your paths beyond tracing out!

Adonai, to that man who pleases you, you give wisdom, knowledge and happiness and the keys to your Kingdom. But to the sinners, you give the task of gathering and storing up wealth to hand it over to the one who pleases you! It is the Spirit in a man, the breath of the Almighty that gives understanding.

Teach me wisdom in the innermost place Almighty God, just as you gave to those four young men: knowledge and understanding of all kinds of literature and learning. For wisdom is more precious than rubies, and nothing we desire can compare with her.

Then, your peace, Shalom, which is beyond our utmost understanding, will keep guard our hearts and thoughts, in Christ Jesus. Change my times and seasons, according to your will Oh LORD, just as you set up kings and depose them. Give wisdom to the wise and knowledge to the discerning.

By your wisdom, you laid the earth's foundations, by your understanding, you set the heavens in place; and your knowledge, the deeps were divided.

Put your law in our minds and write it on our hearts, that we can represent your Kingdom, travelling, preaching and teaching with power and authority!

I will trust in you LORD with all my heart, and lean not on my own understanding; in all my ways, I will acknowledge you, and you shall direct my paths in Jesus' name. Amen.

Shout Hallelujah. The Lord wants you to prosper. As you become more familiar with the prayers, substitute the pronouns "I," "You", and "We" with the names of your loved ones as the LORD leads.

Let us pray…

LORD, we know that you are near to all who call upon you; we are confident that, if we ask anything according to your will, you will hear us, and if we know that you hear us in whatever we ask, we know that we have the requests which we have asked of you. Today, I declare that the eyes of the hearts of God's saints are enlightened that they may know the hope to which He has called them (for the riches of His glorious inheritance in His holy people). For in Him dwells all the fullness of the Godhead bodily; and we are complete in Him, who is the head of all principality and power.

Ephesians 6:12 says we do not wrestle against flesh and blood, but against principalities, against powers, against the rulers of the darkness of this age, against spiritual hosts of wickedness in the heavenly places. The powers that bound people are head quartered in the heavenlies where the prince of the power of the air is enthroned. But the LORD has given us the power to tread on serpents and scorpions, and over all the power of the enemy: and nothing shall by any means hurt us. The Spirit of the LORD gives way to being anointed to preach good tidings unto the meek; bind up the brokenhearted, to proclaim liberty to the captives, and the opening of the prison to them that are bound in Jesus' name. Amen.

Now I release you to go and walk by faith and not by sight. Either you believe or you don't believe in the word of the LORD. For the LORD is a savior to them that believe "If ye had faith as a grain of mustard seed, ye might say unto this sycamore tree, be thou plucked up by the root, and be thou planted in the sea; and it should obey you." Put on and never take off your pieces of armor; loins girth with truth, heart covered with the breastplate of righteousness, feet shod with preparation of the Gospel of peace, having the shield of faith and the sword of the Spirit, which is the word of God, praying the Spirit, and having the head covered with the helmet of salvation.

Now Father, let this message be not just as a teaching but a request from our hearts for you to send your angels to do our biddings in Jesus' Name.

IV

MESSAGES OF ENCOURAGEMENT

I just want to encourage your hearts about kingdom celebration and focus. Renowned Pastor and author Joel Osteen reminds us in one of his quotes that, "when you focus on being a blessing, God makes sure that you are always blessed in abundance."

In the book of Proverbs 11:25-31, it reads:

The liberal soul shall be made fat: and he that watereth shall be watered also himself. He that withholdeth corn, the people shall curse him: but blessing shall be upon the head of him that selleth it. He that diligently seeketh good procureth favour: but he that seeketh mischief, it shall come unto him. He that trusteth in his riches shall fall: but the righteous shall flourish as a branch. He that troubleth his own house shall inherit the wind: and the fool shall be servant to the wise of heart. The fruit of the righteous is a tree of life; and he that winneth souls is wise. Behold, the righteous shall be recompensed in the earth: much more the wicked and the sinner.

While we are focusing on blessing other saints of God, we have to activate spiritual discernment. The Bible tells us to be sober, be vigilant; because our adversary the devil, as a roaring lion, walketh about, seeking whom he may devour (1 Pet. 5:8). We have to pray daily and cover our property, possessions and personage from attacks from the enemy and other negative influences. While you celebrate the purpose you have to fulfill and you're blazing with the zeal to do the work of the LORD, pray that the fire of the Lord bring light to areas of darkness in and around your dwelling. Remember that the tongues of some people devise mischief; like a sharp razor, working deceitfully (Psalms 52:20). Though the Bible declares that nothing by any means can harm us, it does not mean that the enemy will not try. When people see that you are celebrating and covered by the grace and favor of God, this is the time they allow themselves to be used by the devil, especially if they are canal and not spiritual. They do this not for your good and the will of God. There are enemies of Christ (Philippians 3:18-19); this is a fact. If you have Christ in you, then you will have enemies. It is important not to deny the fact that there is a devil that is out to kill, steal and destroy.

King Solomon allowed himself to be influenced by the many wives that he took unto himself. The very people that were close to him caused him to sin. He allowed his wives to worship their own gods, and build altars for them to worship. If you study the word carefully, you will see that this led to division and deterioration. By the time King Solomon's son Rehoboam came to sit on the throne, the kingdom became divided. In this season, we need to seek the Lord's guidance in opening up ourselves to relationships and allowing people to come into our space. Remember that evil communications corrupt good manners (I Cor. 15:33).

When you do not focus solely on God and then place our attention elsewhere, the Lord, after sending warning signs to you, and you're not taking heed to them, He will allow you to fall into the hands of the enemy. Recall what happened when Israel mingled with other citizens of the pagan nations and worshipped other gods. They ended in captivity in Babylon (1 Chron 9:1), leaving the land empty and desolate, and the temple itself destroyed. In this same way, the enemy is set to destroy us.

Do not get me wrong; God is also just. But His kingdom will come on earth and if we do not willfully lend our assistance to His plans, it will go on, but without us. The Israelites were unfaithful to the God of their ancestors and prostituted themselves to the gods of the peoples of the land, whom God had destroyed before them (I Chron 5:25). Do not allow people who are not led by the Spirit of God to speak things into, around or over you.

I want to encourage you to be grounded in Christ and the things of Christ in this hour. The enemy will try to survey your present actions and destroy you at the moment he sees fit; for we wrestle not against flesh and blood, but against principalities, against powers, against the rulers of the darkness of this world, against spiritual wickedness in high places (Eph 6:12). Guard your spiritual fervor. Let no one look down on your youthfulness, but rather in speech, conduct, love, faith and purity, show yourself an example of those who believe (1 Tim. 4:13).

For this you know with certainty, that no immoral or impure person or covetous man, who is an idolater, has an inheritance in the kingdom of Christ and God. Let no one deceive you with empty words, for because of these things the wrath of God comes upon the sons of disobedience. Therefore do not be partakers with them; for you were once darkness, but now you are light in the Lord. Live as children of light (for the fruit of the light consists in all goodness, righteousness and truth) and find out what pleases the Lord. Have nothing to do with the fruitless deeds of darkness, but rather expose them. It is shameful even to mention what the disobedient do in secret. But everything exposed by the light becomes visible and everything that is illuminated becomes a light. This is why it is said: "Wake up, sleeper, rise from the dead, and Christ will shine on you." Be very careful, then, how you live not as unwise but as wise, making the most of every opportunity, because the days are evil. Therefore do not be foolish, but understand what the Lord's will is. Ephesians 5:5-17

In this hour, guard your hearing, your time, your purpose, who you connect with whether old or new friends. In all, be vigilant. Remember when we become comfortable and let our guards down, we open up ourselves for attacks. Apostle Paul told Timothy that, "when we do or connect with others who teach false doctrines or devote themselves to myths that end in genealogies, it promotes controversial speculations rather than advance the kingdom of God." Therefore, our faith becomes wavering.

Our goal as Kingdom citizens with a burning desire for God should be to love, which comes from a pure heart and a good conscience (we should be sensitive, being led by the Spirit) and a sincere faith. Some have departed from these and have turned to meaningless talk. Do we have such people in our midst? Do we have people around us who dwell on power, vengeance, arrogance, hatefulness and manipulation? How close are we to them, how much do they know about our endeavors? The word of God encourages us that whoever keeps his mouth and his tongue keeps himself out of trouble (Proverbs 21:23). "Whoever guards his mouth preserves his life; he who opens wide his lips comes to ruin" (Prov. 13:3).

As we celebrate Jesus Christ our Lord and Savior this season, let us remember His purpose — which is to save us from being eternally separated from God, and so we have no room for error. Strengthen your relationship with Christ and assist in the impartation of His Kingdom. Our call as Christians is too serious for us to become distracted. Study the Word like never before and ask the Holy Spirit to lead you to new revelations.

"So also, when we were children, we were in slavery under the basic principles of the world. But when the time had fully come, God sent his Son, born of a woman, born under law, to redeem those under law, that we might receive the full rights of sons. Because you are sons, God sent the Spirit of his Son into our hearts, the Spirit who calls out, ""Abba", and Father." So you are no longer a slave, but a son; and since you are a son, God has made you also an heir. Formerly, when you did not know God, you were slaves to those who by nature are not gods. But now that you know God— or rather are known by God—how is it that you are turning back to those weak and miserable principles? Do you wish to be enslaved by them all over again? You are observing special days and months and seasons and years!" (Galatians 4:3-10)

There is no room to stop, look back or step away from our call, for we all know from whence we came. The Lord has made us new creations.

Jesus' purpose was to save 'His' people from their sin (Matthew 1:21). As great as Jesus is, as a new born, His parents had to be led by the Spirit in order to keep him safe from danger. The wise men did not reveal where he was. His parents had to flee to Egypt. That is, they moved away from what was familiar to a new place to ensure His protection for a particular time. Your particular time has come to embark into fullness. If Jesus' parents had to be cautious, what do you think about yourself? Think about that for a minute.

Saints of God, it is time for Kingdom celebration. Arise and shine for your light has come. Just as Jesus Christ, let us be about our Father's business; we are His people and the sheep of His pastures, entering His gates with thanksgiving and His courts with praise, thus activating the wisdom of God!

Finally, brothers, whatever is true, whatever is noble, whatever is right, whatever is pure, whatever is lovely, whatever is admirable—if anything is excellent or praiseworthy—think about such things. Whatever you have learned or received or heard from me, or seen in me—put it into practice. And the God of peace will be with you. Philippians 4:8-9

You are the salt of the earth. But if salt loses its flavor, how shall it be seasoned, it is then good for nothing but to be thrown out and trampled underfoot by men. Matthew 5:13

Finally my brethren be strong in the Lord and the power of his might. Ephesians 6:10

Let us be careful that whoever you and I connect with in this season also dwell on these things.

Peace be with you!

V

THE MIGHTY WOMEN OF GOD PRAYER!

Direct my footsteps according to your word oh LORD. Let no sin rule over me. Let me be not conformed to the patterns of this world, but be transformed by the renewing of my mind; for I am to you the pleasing aroma of Christ, among those who are being saved.

Let there be no condemnation for me, a woman who is in you Jesus Christ; a woman who speaks the truth in love; doing everything without complaining, or arguing, to become blameless and humble. For a quarrelsome or complaining woman is like a constant dripping on a raining day; complaining is thanklessness. Let there be no unwholesome words from my mouth, but only what is helpful for building others up according to their needs. Let my utterances be seasoned with grace that it may benefit those who listen. Get rid of all bitterness, rage and anger, brawling and slander, along with every form of malice that is in me. I am not worthy. I will hide your word in my heart and fix my eyes on Jesus the author and finisher of my faith.

Clothe me with strength and honor that I may rejoice in time to come! For I will trust in you, Jehovah Jireh, in all my ways and lean not on my own understanding, acknowledging you will direct my path. Your truth shall cover my loins and your righteousness be my breastplate, and faith my shield. My officers are peace, my walls are salvation and praises are my gates!

Create in me a virtuous wife whose worth is far more than rubies. Let the heart of my husband safely trust me so he will have no lack of gain. Like an apple tree among the trees of the forest, my beloved will be among the young men while I delight to sit in his shade, and his fruit shall be sweet to my taste as he praises me. He shall be known in the gates, when he sits among the elders of the land. Even my children will rise up and call me blessed.

Gird me with strength oh Mighty One and strengthen my arms to willingly work with my hands and provide food for my household and bless others with my profits. For all glory and honor I give unto you who have made all things possible for me and all that you have made is good!

I do not run aimlessly; I do not fight like a man beating the air. My time, my time will be used valuably and for the works of the LORD. For the sluggard craves and gets nothing, but the desires of the diligent are fully satisfied. I myself will not be disqualified for the prize.

Let my light shine before men so that they may see your good works and that my lamp does not go out by night. I can do all things through you who have strengthened me so I will not be afraid of hard times.

Jehovah Tsidkenu, your word says that many daughters have done well, but I will excel them all. Charm is deceitful and beauty is passing, but I will fear the LORD. Whatever is true, whatever is noble, whatever is right, whatever is pure, whatever is lovely, and whatever is admirable; if anything is excellent or praiseworthy, I look for you Elohim to create it in me, in Jesus' name. Amen.

VI

PEOPLE OF PROMISE

A revelation given from the Holy Spirit...

When you are appointed by God to complete a certain work, do not allow anyone to convince you differently. The Gospel is the good news about Jesus Christ our Lord and Savior.

There are some who trouble you and want to pervert the Gospel of Christ but if anyone preaches any other gospel than the gospel of Christ let him be accursed. Galatians 1:7-8

Preach Christ and be Christ-like, your divine purpose is a mandate that came from Christ Jesus, not man. We all know the story of Apostle Paul. Just as he, it does not matter what you used to be. In God, you have been justified by your faith in Jesus.

"The just shall live by faith." (Galatians 3:11)

"Christ has redeemed us from the curse of the law having become cursed for us." (Galatians 3: 13)

As Deuteronomy 21:23 confirms, *"Curseth is he who hangs on a tree."*

"When we were children, we were in bondage under the element of the world but when the fullness of time came, God sent his son to redeem us" (Galatians 4:2). It is God who chose you and you have answered His call. Many out there are in bondage because they do not want to submit to the will of our Almighty God who truly does not want one anyone to perish (2 Pet. 3:0). He has even sent His Holy Spirit to abide in us.

Saints of God, there are many out there who persecute, mock, scoff and do many more of like nature. However, the word of God declares that we should rejoice, break forth and shout (Galatians 4:27). These people are doomed to desolation unless they repent and turn from there wicked ways. I want to remind you that you are of a promise. The word of God says, *"Cast out the* bondwoman and her son, for the son of the bondswoman shall not be heir with the son of the free woman" (Galatians 4:30). Those who are under spiritual bondage and produce evil shall not reign with you; they cannot be in agreement and celebrate with you. There are some people who think they are everything when they are nothing, thus deceiving themselves; people operating illegally against the will of God shall not succeed. Don't be dismayed by these people, you will see them clearly especially during your time of fasting before the Lord.

"The Bible declares that he who troubles you shall bear his judgment whoever he is" (Galatians 5:10).

The acts of the flesh are obvious: sexual immorality, impurity and debauchery; idolatry and witchcraft; hatred, discord, jealousy, fits of rage, selfish ambition, dissensions, factions and envy; drunkenness, orgies, and the like. I warn you, as I did before, that those who live like this will not inherit the kingdom of God. Galatians 5: 19-21

People who usually lay more emphasis on fornication and adultery, etc., must realize that these are not the only things that are sins and of the flesh in operation. What are considered small such as uproars, arguments, disagreement, dispute, strife, dissensions are also sins.

"If you bite and devour one another, be aware lest you consume one another." (Galatians 5:15)

The people who partake in these things will destroy themselves, leave them to God.

"Do not be deceived for God is not mocked whatever a man sows so shall he reap." (Galatians 6:7-8)

This passage talked about the division that was caused by the subject of circumcision. The Holy Spirit showed me that in today's society, in similar fashion, some people because of the class, sect or sub-group, denomination, etc. they belong to will frown upon others. This is because when a person is different from the majority (set apart), it is easier for the popular group (those who are worldly) to mock and downplay the significance of a stance. They criticize and find all sorts of negative issues about the one that is different in order to exalt themselves (boasting in the flesh). In some cases, they have personal issues such as insecurity, identity crisis, home issues, and deception and so on. To take the spotlight off of themselves and make it seem as though they are perfect, they find every fault in others. They call it, 'misery loves company."

"As many as desire to make a good showing in the flesh, these would compel you to be circumcised…but they desire to have you circumcised that they may boast in your flesh." Galatians 6:12-13

Their life is a mess so they want yours to be a mess too. Others do not like them so they don't want anyone to like you. Yet, in some cases, they have no desire and vision for success so they feel you should not walk in your destiny. I submit to you that you don't need the "crowd" to affirm you when you are living a spiritual life, being holy and righteous and pleasing to God. Submit to those who live a spiritual life, especially your spiritual leaders, and follow them as they follow Christ. Drown out their darkness with the fruits of the Spirit because and in due season you shall reap.

"Those who sow in the Flesh they have nothing to reap but corruption" (Galatians 5:8)

As for you when you allow yourselves to be led by the Spirit, your reward is everlasting life. So from this moment on, in the words of Apostle Paul *"Let no one trouble you, for you bear in your body the marks of the Lord Jesus, the grace of our Lord Jesus be with you."* (Galatians 6:17)

"And finally, let him who is taught the word share in all good things with him who teaches. Do not be deceived, God is not mocked; for whatever a man sows, that he will also reap." (Galatians 6:6-7)

Shallaywa Varita Collie

Made in the USA
Columbia, SC
10 November 2024

45703164R00076